TEDDY *B*EAR PHILOSOPHY

TEDDY
BEAR
PHILOSOPHY

*Things My Teddy Bear
Taught Me about Life, Love,
and the Pursuit of Happiness*

Susan E. Schwartz

Photography by Debra McClinton

**Andrews McMeel
Publishing**

Kansas City

www.andrewsmcmeel.com

98 99 00 01 02 TWP 10 9 8 7 6 5 4 3 2 1

Library of Congress Cataloging-in-Publication Data

Schwartz, Susan E. (Susan Einstein)
Teddy bear philosophy : things my teddy bear taught me about life, love, and the pursuit of happiness / Susan E. Schwartz ; photography by Debra McClinton.
     p. cm.
ISBN 0-8362-6784-2 (hd)
1. Teddy bears—Quotations, maxims, etc.
[1. Conduct of life—Quotations, maxims, etc.]
I. Title.
PN6084.C556S39   1998
818'.5402—dc21   98-3336
CIP

ATTENTION: SCHOOLS AND BUSINESSES

Andrews McMeel books are available at quantity discounts with bulk purchase for educational, business, or sales promotional use. For information, please write to: Special Sales Department, Andrews McMeel Publishing, 4520 Main Street, Kansas City, Missouri 64111.

To my brother . . .
who understands what teddy bears are all about
and my mother . . .
who hasn't the slightest idea

Therapists are expensive,
Husbands and wives may stray.
Family can make you crazy,
And friends can move away.
But no matter where you go,
No matter what you do,
Your teddy bear will always be there,
Loving and caring for you.

———

Acknowledgments and Hugs

*B*eing a writer is a solitary profession, which depends only on one's willingness to keep at it. In becoming a published author, however, the writer relies on dozens of people. There are many people I would like to thank without whose help *Teddy Bear Philosophy* would never have come into being. My appreciation goes especially to:

Roseann Sullivan and Suzanne Woo who said, "You should do something with this!" in a very compelling way.

My photographer, Debra McClinton. Deb, your work is music to my eyes. I didn't know how I would find the right person to shoot this project, but I knew right away when I found you. Thanks for going along with the gig those times when neither one of us knew where it was going; those times when you were sure I was headed in the wrong direction; and, especially those times when you were right.

My friend, guide, guardian angel, and emotional tow truck, Susan Page. Susan, without your unfailing inspiration, step-by-step guidance, and willingness to pull me through the goo, *Teddy Bear Philosophy* would still be sitting stuck in some drawer with a lot of other good ideas. I know where I would be without you, Susan, and frankly, I'd rather not think about it.

My agent, Denise Marcil, who is every writer's dream: enthusiastic, responsive, dedicated, determined. I feel incredibly fortunate to have you in my corner.

My editors, Jennifer Fox and Patty Rice. I suggested the extraordinary, asked for the impossible, requested the ridiculous. And you said yes, yes, yes. I could not have created a more supportive editorial team at Andrews McMeel if I designed it myself. Thank you again and again.

Francis Ellis, Lucy Freedman, Amy, Megan, and Rachel Jones, Susan McClinton, Wayne Melton, Susie Robbins, Lou Soucie—thank you for opening your homes, hearts, and businesses to hours of lights, cameras, and chaos.

Joey, Nadya, and Yasmine Abdella, Pam Berkon, Fritz Brauner, Christina, Ken, and Tosca Einstein, Miah McClinton, Nancy McClinton, Penny Markrack, and Melissa, Ryan, Wesley, and Zita Woo—thank you for contributing your time, talent, and teddies.

To the dozens of other people whom Debra and I corralled, cajoled, and captured in film-on-the-fly—you are too numerous to name, but I remember and thank you all.

And then there are those very special people whose contribution extends into every part of my life. My friends: Michael Allen, Nancy Alpert, Joanne Mendes, Kay Pinsker, Channie Steinman, and Nancy Soforenko. Extra hugs to each of you. And most especially, I want to publicly acknowledge my appreciation for my family: Ann, Ken, and Christina Einstein, each of whom has experienced firsthand that my creative expression isn't always limited to the page.

Finally, I want to thank my teddy bears—Cuddles, Roman, Gabriel, Socrates, Hershey, Zero—as well as all the other members of my den, and teddy bears everywhere. The healing, happiness, and divine inspiration you have brought to my life are invaluable. The world needs more like you.

Introduction

When people talk about their first love, they're usually referring to the first person who captured their heart.

My first love was a teddy bear named Cuddles.

Cuddles and I met at a very tender age—I was three, she was even younger. I had just broken my collarbone and felt especially vulnerable. Cuddles was soft, fuzzy behind the ears, and had strange whiskers that didn't seem to belong on her face. I pulled them all out and immediately fell head over heels.

Cuddles and I soon became as one. When I was happy, she was happy. When I suffered, she suffered. She was the model of caring, patience, empathy, and endurance. And with me, she had plenty to endure.

As the years passed, I got to know other bears, but it didn't change things between us. Our relationship became less intense, but I always remembered her and the love and support she had given me.

I had special reason to remember her three years ago. I was preparing to go into the hospital for a difficult surgery and was feeling vulnerable, small, and scared.

"What would help you get through all this more easily?" the doctor asked.

I knew exactly: "A teddy bear!"

Cuddles, then thirty-nine, was still with me, but no longer up to being dragged around. I had to find someone new. Fast.

So the day before I checked into the hospital, I was thinking not about the operation I was about to face, but my need to find a bear. And not just any bear, but The Bear. My soft-stuffed soul mate who would hug me, soothe me, and be there as much as I asked and whenever I needed, just the way Cuddles had.

I spent hours cruising the stores, with no luck. Then, late in the afternoon, a bear caught my eye. He was on the small side and clad in blue-jean overalls. He was a little stiff, yet cuddly and undeniably charming. I hesitated. Was he *the one?* I had always preferred my bears au naturel and had been envisioning a larger bear who had a bit more to hug.

I couldn't let him go, but I couldn't commit, either. It could have been traumatic for both of us, but my new friend understood. I told him I'd make just one more stop.

I walked into a toy store, and there was the bear of my dreams. Soft brown, medium sized, and completely cuddly, wearing nothing but a small brown bow. We hugged, and I was instantaneously smitten. Then, just as suddenly, I felt torn—I was a teddy bear adulterer! I had always been a one-bear person. How could I think of dividing my feelings between two?

I took them both home and tried to decide. Who would be my new, true teddy love?

There was no contest. The decision made itself. It couldn't be either/or; it had to be both. I named the larger one Roman and the smaller one Gabriel.

We went to the hospital together where Roman and Gabriel were all I had hoped they'd be and more. They were loving, caring, nurturing, and best of all, never complained when I asked them to stand in as props or as pillows.

I had a long recuperation period, so the three of us had plenty of time in bed after we came home too. One afternoon, I happened to ask Roman what side of the bed he thought I'd find more comfortable. I didn't really expect an answer, but having asked the question, I felt I should give him the opportunity to respond. When I put his face right next to my ear and listened carefully, he spoke.

"It doesn't matter what side of the bed you sleep on," he said, "as long as you have someone snuggling the other side!"

Well, needless to say, I was astounded. Not at his answer, but that it took me so long to realize how smart teddy bears really are. Since then, I consult with Roman on all my important questions, and he always has something good to say.

It makes me happy to share their wisdom with you in this book. I know if you take time to listen to your teddy, you will find him equally wise.

On the other hand, if you find your teddy bear remains silent, that may be the way he communicates. As Roman says, "Love is a language in which no words say everything."

And that says it all.

Why Teddy Bear *Philosophy?*

*D*o you have a philosophy? Sure you do. It's your way of looking at the world. Your way of explaining to others—and to yourself—why things are the way they are. And why you are the way you are.

It's likely that a variety of influences have contributed to your philosophical development. Family. Friends. Teachers. Your religious training. All of those things have taught you what to believe.

And if you open your mind and your heart, you'll find that there is even more to learn. Every person you meet, every experience you have, everything you come in contact with has the potential to make a contribution to your philosophy of living.

Even your teddy bear.

Yes, even him.

Okay, you say. But why would you want to listen to a teddy bear's philosophy? After all, teddy bears haven't accomplished much. There are no famous teddies in history books. No teddy bear monuments. No bear Halls of Fame. Teddy bears lead very quiet lives. What could you possibly learn from one of them?

The answer is, *a lot*. Because teddy bears are amazingly wise.

I wouldn't be surprised if you didn't know that. (It certainly shocked me!) After all, teddies are renowned for their gentle manner, not their insight. But as it happens, bears are absolutely brilliant.

You see, teddy bears have the ability to discern The Truth—by which I mean, That Which Is Really Important. I'm not sure how they'd fare in solving quadratic equations, but they do have answers to the kinds of questions philosophers have been asking throughout history: What is our purpose? How shall we live our lives? What is the nature of our existence? Stuff like that.

Where does their ability come from? I imagine from their lifelong habit of quiet observation. And their knowledge that inside every complex quandary is a beautifully simple solution waiting to be discovered.

Since I recognized my teddies' gifts, we've had many conversations. I'll share some of them with you here. But there is something very important for you to know: The answers my teddy bears give me may not be the same ones your bears give you. Your teddy will tell you just what you need to hear, when you need to hear it. That's the very best thing about teddy bear philosophy—it is both universal and completely personal.

Teddy bear philosophy has changed my life. I believe it has the potential to change yours—and the world. But you'll have to decide that for yourself.

So, here are some of the things my teddies have taught me about Life, Love, and the Pursuit of Happiness.

LIFE

Just be there.

When I tell my friend Suzanne about my latest life challenges, her first impulse is to want to help me figure out what steps to take to solve the problem. My bear Roman, on the other hand, just wants to give me a hug.

I would hate to hurt Suzanne's feelings, but I like Roman's approach better.

Roman knows he's limited in what he can do, so he doesn't try to do anything. Instead, he's just there with me—listening, loving, hugging, and if I really push him, providing an answer or two.

Teddy bears realize that no matter how much you do, there is always more to be done; but if you can just be wherever you are, and give the moment your full attention, you may find you don't need to do anything else.

Often, just being there is enough.

You've got to be you.

When I asked Roman how he was able to be so happy simply being himself, he looked surprised that I would even think to ask such a question.

"How could I be someone other than me?" he wanted to know.

"I don't know, but lots of people (like me for instance), frequently think their life would be happier if they could only do such-and-such like so-and-so."

"I don't know about So-and-So," Roman replied, "but it seems to me that before you can be someone else, you've got to be who you are. How do you know what you're giving up if you're not aware of what you've got?"

Roman went on to tell me that teddy bears realized their own extraordinary hugging abilities long before anyone else recognized them. "If no one else values your talents, it's all the more reason you should!"

He suggested that instead of focusing on who you want to be, you should spend time appreciating who you are.

After a while, you just may discover the person you most want to be is you!

Look for similarities,
and you will see similarities.

Look for differences,
and you will see differences.

Allow others their point of view.

When I feel that I am right, I am pretty sure that I am right. And even when I'm not, it's still pretty easy for me to feel that I am. (Until sometime later when I find out that, well, maybe I was wrong after all.)

Bears never make those kinds of assumptions. As fuzzy thinkers—the kind that see the world in various shades of brown, instead of in black and white—they avoid thinking in absolutes.

Instead of arguing about who or what is right and wrong, they simply allow that every bear has his own particular point of view, which may be the same—or completely different—from any other bear.

When you think of it, the same thing is probably true for people too.

Of course, I could be wrong.

Your place on the ladder is less important than who you're on it with.

Bears live in an exceptionally egalitarian society. They have no concept of higher status or pulling rank. And they never, ever measure themselves up against each other to see who is softer, fuzzier, more squeezable, or more loved than whom.

To them, all bears (and people) are truly created equal. Big or small, young or old, rare or commonplace, teddies know that they are generally all made of similar stuff. Which, on the one hand, is fairly unremarkable. And on the other, is valuable beyond measure.

"What good is it if some book says you're worth millions, but no one loves you?" Roman asked me. "And if someone loves you very much, as you do, then who cares what anybody says? What could be more important than that?"

"So you're trying to tell me that it doesn't matter where I stack up."

"Well, I just think it's more important to think about who you're stacked up with."

Try to please everyone,
and you end up pleasing no one.

If you're confused about who you are,
chances are others will be too.

Only you know what's true for you.

*I*f I told you I talk to my teddies, you'd probably believe me. But, if I told you my teddies talk back—you'd likely say, "No way!"

But it's true! My teddies do talk to me!

So the question is: Who's right? Do my teddies talk or don't they?

The answer is: We're both right. Or, we're all right. What you believe is what's true for you. And what I believe is what's true for me.

I had a long conversation with my friend Michael who told me that I had to stop talking to my teddies because they're not *real*. I tried to convince him that reality was a matter of opinion, but he didn't agree. I told him that was okay.

Neither Michael nor you need to agree or believe in what's true for me. But you do need to know what's true for you. (Of course, that's just my opinion.) And when you know what's true, don't let anyone try to convince you otherwise.

I'm not suggesting that you should close your head and heart so that once you make up your mind you should never listen to another word someone has to say. But I do believe that you need to listen to that small, still voice inside yourself. The one that tells you things that may not make sense to anyone else, but make all sorts of sense to you.

That's the voice that teddy bears use.

And I believe you should listen to that voice very carefully, because it probably has a very good idea of what's right for you. Even when other people don't agree.

So how do you tell what's The Truth and what's Other Stuff?

Roman and I came up with this list of differences:

♥ You don't really notice The Truth. It's just there.
   Other Stuff keeps trying to draw your attention.

♥ The Truth makes you feel warm, happy, and content.
   Other Stuff makes you feel nervous, edgy, and jumpy.

♥ The Truth allows you freedom.
   Other Stuff holds you down.

♥ The Truth stands beside you.
   Other Stuff tries to lead or push you around.

Roman's final comment on the subject was, "When it's right, you know it."

I agree.

*Some answers are
clearer than others.*

*"Once upon a time, there was a bear.
He said, 'Love and hug everyone.'
The end."*

*Simplicity is
the essence of wisdom.*

We all have something to teach.
And we all have something to learn.

Don't think too much.

"Don't you think it's just a little ironic," I asked Roman, "that after all the reading and studying I've done, I'm taking lessons from a teddy bear?"

"You had to find out how much you don't know."

"Yeah. I've got a lot to learn."

"No. It works the other way. The more you think you know about something, the harder it is for you to learn something new, because your knowledge gets in the way. When you are convinced, as bears are, that you really know nothing, then you have the opportunity to learn a lot."

"Pass that by me again, Romie."

"You can't see what you don't believe is there."

"Okay . . ."

"So the ones who know the least have the most to teach, because they are completely open to whatever they find. That's what makes teddies so wise. Because they truly understand *nothing.*"

"It makes my brain hurt to think about it," I said.

"Mine too," Roman agreed. "The best thing I've learned is to not think too much."

*Never underestimate the benefits
of being a good listener.*

*Life is a balance between
holding on and letting go.*

The best times are when
you can do both simultaneously.

What's up and what's down . . .

. . . largely depends on your perspective.

It helps to be flexible.

What does a teddy bear do when life tosses him a curve? Nothing.

And what does a teddy bear do when things are going swimmingly? Nothing.

What at first glance appears to be inactive indifference is really very active acceptance. It's not that a teddy can't do things differently; he simply doesn't want to. Teddy bears are experts at going with the flow.

"A teddy never knows what his day is going to look like," Roman explained. "You can be snuggling one minute and be flying across the room the next. If you don't stay flexible, you could be in for some very rough landings."

"I suppose I should be a little more careful," I said, rubbing the back of his head.

"Oh, no—it's not a problem," he assured me. "I'd much rather get squished and tossed than just sit on a shelf. But then, I've never done too much shelf time. If I had, I'm sure I'd like that too."

"So teddies are just happy doing whatever?"

"Teddies are happy doing *nothing at all*. The important thing is that, when you're flexible, you can be comfortable wherever you are—whether that's in the middle of things or just watching. And best of all, when you're flexible, you'll always be able to spring back for more."

There may be no accidents,
but there are most certainly mishaps.

Trust that things will be okay.

Hang loose.

When life knocks the stuffing out of you, be sure to put it back in.

*A*n old bear told me this story:

"Many years ago, a particular daddy decided that he didn't want his son playing with me anymore. He was quite certain that it was time to get rid of me. I remember him saying, 'Aren't you a little old for *that?*' And, 'Do you have to bring *that* with you all the time?' (That *that* was me.) But the boy refused to give me up.

"Then, one day, his dad was so angry, he came and ripped me right out of the boy's arms. Split me right down the center. See this scar?" he said, pointing to several inches of stitching from his leg to his neck. "I don't remember it all, but I know I lost a lot of kapok. I thought it was the end. But I was lucky. I never lost my head.

"Of course, the boy rescued me. He picked up all the stuffing he could find, put it back in, and added some other filler on his own. I'm not entirely sure what I've got in there now," he said, looking down. "It doesn't really matter, though. You see, you can't help it if life knocks the stuffing out of you. You just need to remember to put it back in."

Don't overstuff.

The lighter you travel, the more likely you'll be invited to go on the trip.

*Being left alone doesn't mean
that you are being left behind.*

*And being left behind for an afternoon
doesn't mean you are being
left behind forever.*

Remember that you are remembered.

The first time I lost Cuddles, I was five years old and on vacation with my family. I was preparing to take a nap in the backseat of the car, when I reached inside my pillowcase and screamed.

Cuddles was missing.

My father, not an extremely patient person, was quick to imagine the kind of torture that traveling with a hysterical five-year-old could be. He turned the car around and drove back to the hotel we had left half an hour earlier. While he went inside to hunt for Cuddles, my mother, brother, and I waited. And waited. And waited.

When he finally came back, he was empty-handed. "Cuddles wasn't there. Maybe she thought you forgot her."

"Forgot her? How could I forget?!"

I started to wail again, but not for long. As my father turned to slip into his seat, I saw a familiar flash of white fur. He had stuck Cuddles into the back of his pants.

"Don't forget her again," he admonished me while she and I enjoyed a tear-fully happy reunion.

My father never let me forget that story, and years later, when I was at camp, he was still writing to me, "Don't forget to put Cuddles in your pillow . . ."

I heeded his words, and from that day forward, I never let Cuddles out of my sight. She not only went everywhere with me all through childhood, she traveled with me on trips abroad well into my adulthood. There were many close calls, but I never lost Cuddles again.

Until the afternoon when we were shooting her picture for this book.

It was all the more ironic, because my brother had grilled me for several min-utes before he allowed me to take his bears to appear in the same shot. "Where are you going to go?" he wanted to know. "What are you going to carry them in? What are you going to have them do?"

After repeated assurances that I was extremely responsible and wouldn't ask Jingles or Baby Junior to do anything unusual, difficult, or dangerous, he finally gave his consent to let them go. As promised, I brought them home safe and sound.

But my bear, my Cuddles, was missing.

I quickly drove back to my mother's house where we had taken the shot. Everything was back to normal. Our old luggage had been put away, the scene we had set was already a memory. I frantically searched under tables and behind the sofa. No Cuddles.

Where could she be? Where else did I go? Where might I have dropped her?

I sank down to collect my thoughts and then felt something strange tickling me in the back of my pants. Cuddles' small, white body had been camouflaged in the chair's bold brown-and-white print.

"You silly bear! Still up to your old tricks! Did you think I'd forget you?"

As I held her tight, the memory of my father's rescue rushed back in. "Do you remember when Daddy . . ." and then I realized, of course. Of course she does.

The second time I lost Cuddles was August 15—the anniversary of my father's death, thirty years before.

I tucked her inside my sweater for safekeeping. "He'd be glad to know you still remember him," I told her.

She didn't say anything, but I knew what she was thinking: Remember him? Of course I remember him. How could I ever forget?

LOVE

Always be where you can be found.

Before someone can love you he has to meet you.

And before he can meet you he has to be able to find you.

So, it follows that if you want someone to love you, be where you can be found!

Don't sit back on a shelf hoping someone might notice you as they walk by. Don't hide under the covers and pray that someone will happen upon you by accident. Don't play hard-to-get.

Put yourself front and center.

Tie on a bright ribbon.

Smile.

That's what bears do. And it works for them every time.

When you love someone, let them know.

People can be shy or scared to express their love.

Bears never are.

Bears know that love is the most important thing in the world. Without it—or the hope of it—there really is very little reason to get up in the morning. So they express their love as much and as often as possible.

And as for feeling silly . . . or worrying that you won't be loved back . . . or that loving someone suddenly gives you some incredible responsibility . . . Roman says:

"None of those things ever occur to me. I just know that being loving makes me feel good, and it seems to make others feel good too. If I weren't loving, I wouldn't have those good feelings. That's why I do it."

Seems like a good reason we should do it too.

"I love you" is a statement,
not a question.
It doesn't require a response.

Allow yourself to be adored.

Among teddy bears' extraordinary abilities is the way they so easily allow themselves to be adored.

What's so hard about that?

Well, I don't know about you, but I feel very uncomfortable when someone tells me that I'm cute and sweet and wonderful. (Not that it happens so often.) Maybe it's just me, but I always suspect they want something. So instead of enjoying their compliments, I shift and squirm, waiting for the punch line. Not surprisingly, the line of people who want to hug and kiss and compliment me is rather short.

Roman, on the other hand, never tires of hearing how special he is, how much he is loved, and how important he is to me. In fact, he loves it. So I keep telling him. And then I tell him some more.

Now, when Roman covers me with kisses and says how much he loves me, I just take it in. I haven't had a lot of people trying to squeeze and hug me yet, but I'm doing my best to be ready in case they ever do.

Love leaves an impression.

Hold on to what you love.

*I*n the '60s, people used to say that if you love something, you should let it go. My teddy bear philosophers disagree.

They say that if you love something, you should hold on to it. Honor it. Devote time and space to it. Keep it in a special place in your heart and soul so that it is always close to you.

To be quite honest, I initially balked at their suggestion.

"Roman, people aren't like teddy bears. Some people need space. They start to feel claustrophobic when someone is holding on too tight."

"Not if you hold someone in your heart," Roman said. "The person may not always be there, but if you honor, care for, and love her, you can still feel like she is. Most of the time, you're not *really* there with me, but since you have a permanent place in my heart, I always feel like you are."

"So you take the love with you, not the person."

"Well, it is nicer to have both," Roman admitted. "But if I had to make a choice, I'd rather have full-time love with a part-time person than a full-time person with just part-time love."

Yeah, Romie. Me too.

*It's easier to recognize attraction
than try to explain it.*

Don't let anyone tell you who to love.

Your little imperfections
are what make you . . . you.

$\mathscr{I}$ was wandering through a local department store when I came across teddy bear backpacks. I had to have one.

Knowing bears as I do, I couldn't just choose the first one I saw. I had to sit them down all together and meet them one-by-one.

One had a crooked smile. Another's head was sewn on slightly askew. The third had a rakish tilt to his bow tie. And the last one had no obvious defects. He was perfect.

Now, you might think that the perfect one was the obvious one to choose, but personally, I found him a little boring. After several minutes of concentrated decision making, I chose the crook-necked one, much to my mother's consternation.

"Why would you want *that* one?" she moaned, obviously distressed that even when it came to teddy bears, I was incapable of making a suitable choice.

I couldn't give her a solid rational reason why Socrates (as I later named him) appealed to me far more than the others had, but I suppose the fact that he wasn't absolutely perfect set him apart in some way. It showed that he was an individual—that had his own personality. I like that in a bear.

And oddly enough, I've found I prefer that in people too.

It used to be that when someone asked me about the man I'd like to meet, I'd say I wanted him to be tall, dark, and handsome . . . and I'd envision the perfect prince who'd sweep me off my feet.

But then I discovered that the people I really found attractive didn't fit that description—or any one description—at all. They were all different. The only thing they had in common was that each had his own little quirks and qualities that made him special to me.

So now if someone wants to know about the kind of man I'd like to meet, I say: If he's warm, fuzzy, and not too perfect, he'll probably be perfect for me.

Love comes wrapped
in all kinds of packages.

Keeping the bed warm is a wonderful gift.

Giving someone the space he needs is a gift.

. . . and so is giving time to share.

*There's no way to know
how love will look,
but you can know how it will feel.*

Love feels good.

How do you know when someone really loves you?

Is it because they call you ten times a day or shower you with gifts? Is it because they send you cards and flowers? Rub your back? Take your dog for a walk?

Do they have to actually say it? And if someone does say *I love you,* does that mean they really do?

How do you know?

"How do you know when someone loves you, Roman?"

"I don't know. You're the only one who ever has."

"Well, how do you know that I love you?"

"I never questioned it," he said. "I would say you know someone really loves you when you don't feel you have to ask and wonder if they do."

*You can't measure love
in ounces and pounds.*

———

Don't even try.

Enjoy all the love you have.
Take all the love you can get.

Since we live in a world that measures everything in terms of big and small, high and low, or up and down, when someone says *I love you*, it's natural to want to know just how *much* they do.

But why? I never think of asking Roman how much he loves me. I don't keep track of how much or how often we hug. I don't wonder who said nicer things to whom. I don't calculate how much time we spend snuggling. Or even notice how long we've been together.

Because I know quantity can't measure feelings.

Because I know Roman loves me.

Because, okay, Roman is a bear.

But actually, people aren't all that different.

Love of any kind is too weighty to be measured on any scale. And too precious to be valued in any currency. It is too tremendous to fit into any box; too incredible to be defined by any words.

So rather than trying to weigh and measure how much someone loves you, why not just enjoy experiencing the fruits of love instead?

Then, you may notice as Roman did, "The best thing about love is that you can always squeeze out a little more." However much that may be.

There's no such thing
as too many hugs.

Sometimes, it's even nice
to be smothered.

*There are times when being
small and squishy
is preferable to being
big and strong.*

―――――

*It's easier to get close to someone
when there are no hard edges.*

Everybody has a soft spot somewhere.

Love accommodates.

*I*t's not that easy being a teddy bear. After all, you have to tolerate being dragged around, tossed aside, squished, scrunched, and slept on (maybe even drooled on), all for nothing more than a few good hugs.

It's a lot like a lot of relationships.

The big difference is that teddy bears don't just tolerate being dragged and squished, they *enjoy* it.

I asked Gabriel, since he's the one who most often serves pillow duty, how he's able to be so constantly supportive without complaint.

"I didn't realize that I was being *supportive!*" he said with a satisfied grin. "To me, that's just how we sleep together!"

"It's all the same thing," Roman agreed. "Whether you're hugged, squished, dragged, or carried, the important thing is that you're together—not what you're doing."

"That's fine for teddy bears," I said. "But most people want to feel that they get as good as they give."

"That's funny," Roman said. "I always feel like I get when I give."

"Oh, Romie," I sighed. "I'll never be as sweet and pure and loving as you."

"Really? To tell you the truth, I hadn't noticed."

There's nothing wrong with
being a little messed up.

Familiarity breeds content.

It doesn't matter what side
of the bed you sleep on
as long as you have someone
snuggling the other side.

Love is a language
in which no words
say everything.

In order to hear it
you must listen
through your heart.

HAPPINESS

You get a great view
from the top . . .
but it's a lot more fun
in the middle.

Establish a habit of "bearing up."

*S*urveys (very informal surveys) have shown that people who develop an early habit of *bearing up*—that is, using a bear to alleviate stress—lead longer, happier, healthier lives than those who don't.

Research on the effect of bearing up is still being conducted; however, preliminary results offer several theories to explain the difference in longevity between teddy bear and non–teddy bear owners. Among them: People who do not reach for a teddy bear when under stress frequently seek much-less-healthful alternatives. (You know the ones we mean.) Teddy bear owners are frequently hugged, soothed, and cuddled, while their non–teddy bear counterparts are frequently irritated, aggravated, and annoyed. In addition, teddy bear owners are always surrounded by friends, while non-owners frequently feel isolated.

Anecdotal evidence also shows that bears have extraordinary healing powers. This explains why teddy bears are among the first supplies requested after major disasters.

To this researcher, the conclusion is obvious: *Bearing up* significantly reduces the likelihood of breaking down!

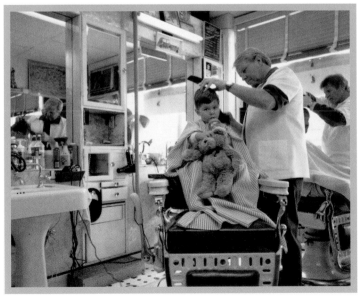

He who says he has
no need of a bear . . .

is the person who needs one most.

*Loneliness ends where
reaching out begins.*

Software will never replace a soft bear.

*The truly important things in life
never become outdated, outmoded,
or obsolete.*

Fuzzy logic has a logic all its own.

*O*nce upon a time, I was married to a computer scientist who was fond of reminding me that my arguments didn't make a lot of sense. I was basing everything on *emotions,* he used to tell me. Try thinking *logically.*

Well, I tried it and I didn't like it.

To my way of thinking, the world seems like a very limited place when you look at it in terms of *if* you do this, *then* that will happen. The way I see it is *if* you do this, *then* anything's possible!

Some people call that kind of thinking "fuzzy logic" and when they say it, you know they think there's something wrong with it.

But I say, fuzzy logic has a logic all its own.

Fuzzy logic is the willingness to bend or even break the rules—to be creative and think outside the box. Fuzzy logic says that there are things beyond our understanding—like getting wisdom from teddy bears—that are meaningful, real, and important even if we can't explain how they work or why.

It may be "fuzzy logic," but Roman and I agree that it makes all sorts of sense to us.

Spend time with people who understand you.

*I*n the course of your lifetime, you'll meet all sorts of people. Some will feel like long-lost mates minutes after you meet. Others, you'll know all your life and never quite have the feeling that they see the real you.

It's good to make acquaintances with lots of different types. But only share your heart and dreams with friends who truly understand you.

Like your teddy bear.

Your teddy bear not only understands, but accepts, supports, and adores you exactly the way you are. With his help, you can find people who will love you just as fully and unconditionally as he does. Here's how:

When you're out with your beloved teddy, some people will ask about him, agree about how wonderful he is, and share their own bear stories with you. Those are the kind of people you want to get to know.

Under the same circumstances, others will do their very best to ignore your teddy, or if that's not possible, ask you, "What's with the bear?" You may have the urge to explain, but you really needn't bother. Those people are not bad or mean or wrong; they simply do not understand.

It's good that it takes all kinds of people to make a world. But it's even better to spend time with the kind of people who want to make the same kind of world as you.

Open your home to friends.

Party, party, party.

Wait for an occasion to celebrate and you can wait a long time. But get together with a friend who loves you and you can have a party anytime for any reason.

Or better yet, no reason at all.

Teddy bear picnics. Teddy bear teas. Teddy bear pajama parties.

Roman's favorite is a party of two.

I'm especially fond of that one too.

Get as many hugs as you can every day. Plus one more.

*L*ike water, food, and sleep, hugs are a daily essential. As is true with those other basics, you can live without sufficient hugging . . . but not well, and not for long. (Of course, you don't need a teddy bear to tell you that.)

How many hugs do you need? Is there a minimum daily hug requirement? Is one good hug enough? What about just a quick squeeze?

I looked for reference material on the subject, until I realized that I had my own resident expert on hand.

"We all need all the hugs we can get," was Roman's response. "The more, the better."

"But if a person can't or doesn't get a hug every day, that's okay?"

"No! No! That's why whenever you get a hug, you should always get just one more, as an extra, to keep for those times when you really need a hug, and there's no one around."

So be sure to put your teddy where he will best remind you to get your daily hugs. And remember: If, for some reason, your teddy bear is not available, you can always hug people too.

Use your common scents.

Bears, as you may know, have a very acute sense of smell. And teddies have inherited that characteristic. Can just a whiff of something make you happy? Roman says so. Here are a few things on his list of favorite smells:

spring flowers

newly mowed grass

sheets just out of the dryer

the air after it rains

bread baking

logs burning in the fireplace

clover honey

peppermint tea

hot chocolate

and (he said I had to say it)—me

Remember what's important.

Why do lots of kids who cherish their teddies leave them behind as adults?

"They forget," Roman said, very quietly. "They forget."

He didn't elaborate, but I think I know what he means.

As people get older, they forget how much fun it is to play. Not how to go on vacation or buy new toys, but how to really play. How to use their imagination. Make up stories. Invent games.

They forget how to be spontaneous. And how nice it is to relax. To let time go by with no point or purpose. To just enjoy doing nothing.

And they forget what's most important of all—sharing love.

"I know what you mean," I told Roman. "I forget, too, sometimes."

"Yes, you do," he said. "Lucky I'm always here to remind you."

Men are from Mars.
Women are from Venus.
Teddy bears are from Heaven.

Embrace whatever comes next.